VOLUME IV

▲▲▲

The Native American Book of

Wisdom

▼▼▼

NATIVE PEOPLE ▲ NATIVE WAYS ▲ SERIES

VOLUME IV

▲▲▲

The Native American Book of

Wisdom

▼▼▼

TEXT BY

White Deer of Autumn

ILLUSTRATIONS BY

Shonto W. Begay

▲ Beyond Words Publishing, Inc. ▲

Published by
Beyond Words Publishing, Inc.
13950 NW Pumpkin Ridge Road
Hillsboro, Oregon 97123
Phone: 503-647-5109
To order: 1-800-284-9673

Page Layout: The TypeSmith
Cover Design: Soga Design

Printed in the United States of America
Distributed by Publishers Group West

Library of Congress Cataloging-in-Publication Data
White Deer of Autumn.
    The native American book of wisdom / text by White Deer
of Autumn ; illustrations by Shonto W. Begay.
        p.   cm. — (Native people, native ways series ; v. 4)
    Summary: A collection of stories focusing on the spiritual and
medicine man traditions of the Native American.
    ISBN 0-941831-73-6 (v. 4) : $4.95
    1. Indians of North America—Religion and mythology—
Juvenile literature.   2. Indians of North America—Medicine—
Juvenile literature.   [1. Indians of North America—Religion
and mythology.   2. Indians of North America—Medicine.]
I. Begay, Shonto W., ill.   II. Title.   III. Series: White Deer
of Autumn. Native people, native ways series ; v. 4.
E98.R3W48   1992
299´.7—dc20   92-17002
                                                              CIP
                                                               AC

*Dedicated to all the elders
who kept the belief and the wisdom alive
and to all of you who will
carry them on*

CONTENTS

PART I

From the Great Mystery: Wakan-Tanka

▼▼▼

CHAPTER 1

Escape from Education

We were "savages," and all who had not come under the influence of the missionary were "heathen," and Wakan-Tanka, who had since the beginning watched over the Lakota and his land, was denied by these men of God.

— from *Land of the Spotted Eagle*,
by Luther Standing Bear

▼▼▼

"Y ou were told not to come back to classes until your hair was cut," Mrs. Henshaw scolded.

Jamie stood at his desk before speaking. It was the rule. "I don't want to cut my hair."

"I don't care what you want," she replied. "That's the rule."

"But . . . I'm Indian."

Mrs. Henshaw breathed loudly. Her lips pressed together. "And what is that supposed to mean?"

Jamie just shrugged his shoulders. He glanced down at his desk. A small spider skittered across the slippery surface. He didn't know what being Indian meant—at least he didn't know how to say it with words.

"What are you looking at?" she demanded. "What's on your desk?"

He looked up. The spirit light his mom always saw sparkling in his black eyes was nearly gone. Since the death of his parents in a car accident just before his fifth birthday, the twinkling spirit light had been fading.

After the funeral, the state had taken custody of Jamie's life. He was moved from one foster home to another. His brown skin and long hair seemed to make adults uncomfortable. Most foster parents felt he might be a bad influence on other kids, so they sent him away. At age twelve he wound up at Big Rock Boarding School, and now he stood fearfully before Mrs. Henshaw. His deep brown hair, parted in the middle, hung past his shoulders. By now, everyone in the class was looking at him.

"It's just a book," he said.

Mrs. Henshaw marched down the aisle to Jamie. When she passed some of the kids, it felt like a wind followed her. Pencils rolled from the desks and onto the floor. Papers blew into the aisle.

She picked up the book. It was well-worn. The front cover was gone, but the words on the first page were still

there. "To Jamie. Love, Dad." Mrs. Henshaw saw only the page Jamie had marked. Staring at her was a picture of Sitting Bull. His hair was braided to his waist. He had no smile — just a stare from his eyes.

"There are many other Indians in this school, Jamie. They don't have to look like this." She pointed at the picture. "Civilized boys don't look like this. You want to live in the past, and you can't." Staring down at Jamie, she sneered at the sight of the spider on the desk. All eight of its tiny legs were frozen still, as if it were trying not to be noticed. Suddenly, she slammed the book shut and dropped it back onto the desk, crushing the tiny creature. Still sneering, she reached into her dress pocket, searching around. She pulled out a small black purse, removed two dollar bills, and threw them onto the desk. "I'll give you one more chance. That's the money for a haircut. Now don't come to school tomorrow without one, or . . . so help me, I'll cut it myself!"

The next day Jamie walked slowly into the classroom, staring at his shoelaces. His deep brown hair hung past his shoulders. Mrs. Henshaw ordered him to the front of the room. She pulled a large pair of scissors from her desk. With each clump that fell to the floor, her smile brightened. "Now you look civilized."

Jamie died a little. Hardly a trace of spirit light shimmered in his dark watery eyes.

"This is how boys should look," she declared when she had finished.

Jamie said nothing. He wondered to himself why Jesus had long hair. Would Mrs. Henshaw have cut his hair too? He began to see that learning about God and civilized people was not going to be easy.

The preacher, and even some of the teachers, told him to watch out for the devil. "He'll make you sin," they said. He learned that God gets angry and will punish a boy for committing sins. And if Jamie didn't learn what the sins were called, the teachers beat him with a belt.

Jamie was forced to go to Sunday-school class. He learned that man was made in God's image. The teacher explained that God lived in Heaven with angels and saints and good Christians and that Heaven is a place where the streets are paved with gold.

The teacher said that Indians who don't accept his faith were heathens. Sinners and heathens don't go to Heaven when they die. Jamie wondered about the souls of his parents.

All the while, his hair kept growing back, like those tough native plants that persist in growing, even through cracks in city sidewalks. Each time Mrs. Henshaw would cut it off.

It was Jamie's turn to read aloud from the Bible, "Be fruitful and multiply, and fill the earth and subdue it." He paused and swallowed hard. "Have dominion over the fish of the sea and over the birds of the air. . . ." He couldn't go on.

He was given a week of detentions. It really wasn't so bad because he got to be alone. Really, he had already been alone, only this time there was no one else around.

It was the word *subdue* that haunted him. It echoed the whole time in his head. He looked it up. "To rule over by

force," he read. Suddenly, it all began to make sense. How else could some people destroy the land I love, he thought, and not be punished by God? He didn't understand.

A few weeks later, Jamie ran away from Big Rock. Mrs. Henshaw watched from her classroom window as he walked out the gate. Before she could think about sounding the alarm, he was running down the road.

CHAPTER 2

Feelings Without Words

Broneco knew there is something about the hill, but he doesn't know what it was. He knew that he will find a cheerfulness there, but still didn't know what kind of happiness.

—from *Miracle Hill*, by
Emerson Blackhorse Mitchell

▼▼▼

S omehow Jamie managed to make his way south. One day he found himself, alone and hungry, on a beach in Florida, gazing far off at the blue ocean. All at once, like a storm releasing itself, he fell to the earth, crying like he had never cried before. It seemed as if a lifetime of pain and sorrow had suddenly risen to the surface. The death of his parents, the beatings at school, and those humiliating days when Mrs. Henshaw cut his hair had all finally taken their toll. For some time, he lay upon the land, weeping from a place deep within himself.

Then, as if waking from some horrible nightmare, his sobbing stopped. He no longer trembled. All he felt now was the earth. It was soft and warm beneath him.

"Mother," he whispered, his face pressed against the ground, "I love you." He remembered that his dad and mom had called the earth Mother. "I've always loved you!" For the first time, Jamie realized that he was not without a mother.

He felt a oneness with the Earth and all the natural things he saw. The ocean, the all-covering sky, the tall, waving sea oats and grasses, and even the weeds, in some mysterious way, shared a part of him, and he a part of them. He knew he was Indian, but he still didn't have words to explain it.

CHAPTER 3

Nippawanock

Longing to be an Indian because his "half-breed" stepfather had more dignity and bearing than anyone else in the town of Pitcher, he existed in neither world. Many years later when his mother "confessed" the guilty secret that his great-grandfather was a Cherokee, Nippawanock knew why he had always "felt" Indian.

> —from *Literature of the American Indian,* by Thomas E. Sanders and Walter W. Peek

▼▼▼

That evening Jamie went to a shopping mall. His stomach ached from hunger. He searched the mall for telephones. Checking the coin-deposit box of each, he managed to collect forty-five cents.

He didn't see the gray-headed man walk up behind him. When Jamie finally noticed, it was too late. He asked the man if he was under arrest. The elderly man just smiled.

"Where are your parents?" the man asked.

He has kind eyes, Jamie thought. "They're dead."

"Where do you live?"

Jamie just shrugged his shoulders. He didn't live anywhere.

"You look hungry. Have you eaten today?"

"No. I think I ate yesterday," Jamie confessed.

"Why don't we find a place here in the mall and get you something to eat?" the man said. Soon Jamie was sitting at a booth in a restaurant, gobbling down chicken, beans, and bread.

"You're an Indian," the man said after Jamie finished.

"Yes."

"Good. So am I. My name is Nippawanock, but you can call me Nip."

"Mine's Jamie."

In the Narragansett-Wampanoag language, *Nippawanock* means "Star That Rises to Greet the Dawn," or "Dawn Star." Although the elder Nippawanock was Cherokee, he was adopted and made a citizen of the Wampanoag Nation.

Nip adopted Jamie.

The practice of adoption is not uncommon among Indians. It's the same as an immigrant coming to the United States to be a citizen, but there is a difference: Indians include all parts of a person's life when making

him or her a citizen. This includes values and beliefs, as well as a pledge of loyalty and belonging.

In any case, Jamie, searching for his identity, had found an uncle. The aging, wise Nippawanock, needing to pass his knowledge to the next generation, had found a nephew. Jamie, with Uncle Nip's help, was about to find words for his feelings about life and about being Indian.

CHAPTER 4

How Much Indian Are You?

▲▲▲

Our people are ebbing away like a rapidly receding tide that will never return. The white man's God cannot love our people or He would protect them.

> — from "The White Man Will Never Be
> Alone," by Chief Sealth (Seattle) of
> the Suquamish and Duwamish tribes

▼▼▼

Uncle Nip's first task was to get Jamie back in school. "You can best serve your people with an education," Uncle Nip said.

Jamie didn't want to go back to school—any school. But Nip insisted.

"Stay away from fighting," Uncle Nip advised his nephew. "Study and earn your diploma, so that you can help the People in that way."

But the young are always quick to fight, and the old to say no. One day, Jamie was shoved by the school bully, Leroy Puckett. "Just how much Indian are you?" Leroy demanded.

The question always bothered Jamie. He gave the standard response, the one that seemed to satisfy most anyone who had asked before. "I'm half," he said.

"If you're only half Indian, you're not even full-blooded! Ahh." He laughed jeeringly in Jamie's face. "You're only a half-breed! You're no Indian." Jamie slugged him before taking a beating himself.

Jamie was suspended for two days for starting a fight. In a way he had started it, but Leroy's words had really bothered him. He waited in the principal's office for Uncle Nip to come get him. For the first time he thought, I'll always be part Indian, never all. He could hardly swallow the bitter taste of such a notion — to be only part of something. Suddenly, he felt empty and alone again.

The Heart Knows What It Is

▲▲▲

I had a Commanche mother and an Irish father. But I'm Commanche. I'm not Irish. . . . When the Commanche took in someone, he became Commanche. He wasn't part this, part that. He was all Commanche or he wasn't Commanche at all. Blood runs the heart. The heart knows what it is.

> —LaDonna Harris, in *Literature of the American Indian*, by Thomas E. Sanders and Walter W. Peek

▼▼▼

When they got home, Uncle Nip made Jamie sit at the table. For a long time, he said nothing to his nephew. Finally he spoke.

"What did chiefs like John Ross, Osceola, Joseph, and Quannah Parker have in common?" Nip asked. Jamie had learned to respect the powers of his uncle. He never knew how Nip could know exactly what he was thinking, but Nip did.

"They were Indian leaders, Uncle." It was an easy answer, but that was Uncle Nip's way of luring you in. Just when you thought you knew something — *pow!* — came the realization that you didn't!

"Yes they were, Jamie, but more important is to know that they were all children of parents who were both Indian and white.

"Now, do you think Chief John Ross was part Cherokee because by blood he was only one-sixteenth Cherokee?" Jamie shook his head. Uncle Nip went on. "Or Osceola, whose English name was Billy Powell — was he part Seminole because of the white blood of his father? How about Chief Joseph, who fought off four divisions of the United States Army with a handful of warriors, women, and children? Do you think his people said you can't lead the Nez Perce because you're only part Indian? And Quannah Parker, the great Commanche leader — do you think his people said you can't lead us because you've got the blood of a white mother in your veins?"

Nippawanock's face smiled confidently. Not his mouth or eyes, but his face. It wasn't a joyous smile, but an affectionate, penetrating one. That's what showed while his old eyes searched for signs that Jamie understood.

"Jamie," he said, "point to the half of you that's Indian."

Jamie felt foolish. Here he was trying to become older. Now he felt like a little boy again, struggling to learn something Uncle Nip must think is quite simple.

"I can't, Uncle."

"But you said you were half Indian. Now which half is it? Your upper half or lower? Back half or front?" This time Nip's lips smiled, and so did those old eyes. His nephew smiled too, foolishly. "You either are or you're not, kid. What does your heart say?"

Jamie paused. "It says I can't be anything but an Indian."

"Then, that's what you are."

"But why does my heart say that, Uncle?"

"Because somehow your birth did not give you a choice. And because you love your Mother Earth and know you are part of the Great Mystery. These are the traditional beliefs that Native Americans have always had."

CHAPTER 6

The Great Mystery

The original attitude of the American Indian toward the Eternal, the "Great Mystery" that surrounds and embraces us, was as simple as it was exalted. To him it was the supreme conception, bringing with it the fullest measure of joy and satisfaction possible in life.

—from *The Soul of the Indian,* by
Ohiyesa (Dr. Charles Eastman)

▼▼▼

It was the first time Jamie had ever heard the words *Great Mystery.* But that was it! It was what he had always felt but could never describe. He didn't have anything against God. He just didn't feel that the idea of God, as certain people described "Him," belonged to the

"Indian" feelings he had about life. God, his Sunday-school teacher said, lived in Heaven and was in the image of man. Mrs. Henshaw had told them that God couldn't be in everything. God, as Jamie had learned, couldn't be in spiders, or people wouldn't be so quick to kill them. Jamie had always felt that something special dwelled in all things, connecting them into some unimaginable oneness that always was and always would be.

And it couldn't be the "Great Spirit" that he had heard others use to explain what Native Americans believed. As Uncle Nip explained, you don't really know that the source of life and of all things is spirit.

"*Spirit* is a word that defines what something is, Jamie. The Great Mystery is beyond explaining. It is, indeed, the Great Mystery!"

Nip explained how older Indians, not very familiar with the English language, would sometimes refer to the *First Cause* as the Great Spirit. "For them," he said, "the only word in English that could describe what connects all things and gives life to them is *spirit*. The sum total of all spirit living together at this moment, to them, would be the Great Spirit."

For these reasons, the name Great Mystery made so much sense to Jamie, so much extraordinary and simple sense. This name described the way he felt things were connected.

Nip continued, "The Iroquois called the Great Mystery *Sakoiatisan*. The Ojibwa called the Mystery *Kitche-Manitou*. *Kitche* means something very great, and

Manitou means something that has spirit, or rather a holy mystery power.

"Like the Sioux, or Lakota, who addressed *Wakan-Tanka* in their prayers and songs, each Native American nation and tribe had a name for the Great Mystery. *Wakan,* in Lakota, is something very holy, in a mysterious and sacred way, and *Tanka* is something very great, or an immense importance."

It was difficult even for Uncle Nip to translate a concept as abstract as Wakan-Tanka, the Great Mystery, into English. *Abstract* is something of the mind, like an idea. "One must know English as well as Native thinking to translate from one language to another," he said. "The best and most accurate translation of the different Native American names for the Giver of Life, the First Cause of All, is the Great Holy Mystery.

"It is your awareness, Jamie, that the Great Mystery is part of you and that you are part of the Mystery which gives you identity. It's what makes a person a Cherokee or Ojibwa or Cheyenne or Hopi or Seminole or simply a Native American: That feeling is knowing you share the Great Mystery of life with all things. This understanding, together with your love for Mother Earth, is what makes you whole."

"Then there is no such idea as being part Indian, is there, Uncle?"

"You can be of Indian descent," he answered, "but you can't be part Indian. The heart knows what it is, Jamie. And either you are or you aren't."

CHAPTER 7

Body, Spirit, Ghost

▲ ▲ ▲

A wolf
I considered myself,
But the owls are hooting
And the night
I fear.

— A song of the Teton Sioux

"I think I'm afraid to die, Uncle."

"And why would an Indian be afraid to die? After all, what happens to the body after death?"

"It's usually buried or cremated."

"And where does it go, Jamie?"

"In the earth."

"Now, what could be so awful about having our bodies return to our Mother Earth? I agree that it's not a pleasant thought, thinking about becoming food for other life-forms, but the body doesn't die that way. It simply changes form."

"What about Heaven, Uncle? Do Indians have a 'happy hunting ground' where we go, like I've heard some people say?"

Uncle Nip thought hard for a moment. "Our traditional beliefs say that there are three parts to a human being: body, spirit, and ghost. At death, our bodies return to Mother Earth to nourish what has nourished us. This is giving something back after all we've taken from her.

"Even the spirit, which belongs to the Great Mystery, returns to its source. Some of our people say this journey takes place on a path of stars. Others describe the spirit's return to the Great Mystery as a drop of water falling into the ocean—it becomes a part of everything again as the light of a candle becomes one with the fire of the sun. That's why we can sometimes feel our loved ones in the warm air, or hear them in a bird's song, or even sense them in the wind.

"Now the ghost is another thing," he continued. "The ghost part of ourselves is the nonphysical form of our bodies. There are stories of a ghost world and a great river that our ghosts must cross to enter it. Some Indians say they have seen this world and that it is very beautiful. I have not. I have seen ghosts. They are of the land and can appear in times of need, for good or bad reasons. But the ghost cannot harm. It can console the living. Sometimes it's a voice you hear in your mind; other times it's a reflection in your mind." At this point, Uncle

Nip asked his nephew to look briefly at a light bulb. "Now close your eyes," he said. "Can you still see the image of the light?"

Jamie nodded.

"That's like the ghost," Nip said.

"At death, it's not the ghost of the loved one we address, but the spirit. We want to encourage it to go back to where it came from, back to the Great Mystery. If a person has filled his or her life with good, all that good pours back into the Great Mystery for the living and for future generations.

"You see, it was the spirits and bodies of past elders, women, and warriors who returned to the Mystery and to Mother Earth that enabled our children to be born with such strong spirit today. For this reason, they still have that special love for the land. For loving and living good lives, like your parents, in balance with the Earth and in harmony with nature, they poured much goodness back. Some of it poured into you.

"Now, granted, I could think of ways I wouldn't want to die. But really, do you still think death is an awful thing?"

Jamie shook his head. "No, I guess not."

Uncle Nip laughed. "There is an old Indian saying: 'That which the children of the earth do not understand as they walk the path of life will become clear to them only when they pass into the Great Mystery of Wakan-Tanka.' In other words, what you and I don't understand about the Great Mystery now, we will understand when our spirits return to it."

CHAPTER 8

Everything Is Equal

▲▲▲

Behold, my brothers, the spring has come; the earth has received the embraces of the sun and we shall soon see the results of that love!

Every seed is awakened and so has all animal life. It is through this mysterious power that we too have our being and we therefore yield to our neighbors, even our animal neighbors, the same right as ourselves, to inhabit this land.

— Sitting Bull, in *Touch the Earth*,
by T. C. McLuhan

"Sometimes I wish I weren't so different, Uncle. I mean I wish Indians could believe the way we want and not have to feel so . . . different."

Uncle Nip had no affection for missionaries, and he would use any chance to express that. "If the missionaries who seek to make converts of Native Americans would consider more carefully how different their beliefs are from the beliefs which sprang from this land, then they would better understand Native Americans.

"In the Bible's Story of Creation, God says, 'Be fruitful and multiply, and fill the earth and subdue it; and have dominion over the fish of the sea and over the birds of the air and over every living thing that moves upon the earth.'

"To us, the idea that we should 'subdue' the earth and have dominion over all her children is unthinkable."

Uncle Nip paused. "Yes, you are different, Jamie. But be proud of that difference, not ashamed! You are not wrong to believe that humans should not subdue their Mother, the Earth.

"Why, to subdue the earth is as far away from Native thinking as one can get. And to think that we should control the lives of our elder animal, insect, and plant relatives would be to believe that we are superior to them. No Indian ever felt that he was better or more important than they are."

Jamie began to learn the American Indian way. Nip explained that all things are equal in the Mystery, because all things share the Mystery together, including men and women. The Great Mystery is both male and female, so many Native Americans think of the Sky, or sometimes of the Sun, as Father, and the Earth as Mother. These are the male and female qualities of the Great

Mystery. Both are equally important, although each has a different role.

He said that in Native belief, the Sky is the protector and provider. We know that without Father Sky we would die. Without his protection, the rays of the sun would burn us up. Think about the recent discovery of holes in the ozone. It has become a worldwide concern because scientists know the importance of ozone. Without that protective shield, people would grow sick and die. Most other life-forms would die too. We also know that the Sky provides rain. Without the rain to give us water, we would all die. And are not seeds carried by the wind across the Sky?

"The Earth," he said "then accepts or rejects the seeds. Those she accepts, she nurtures. This includes us, as Mother Earth provides all the foods we eat and the medicines to keep us healthy. She takes care of her children — all of them, not just the humans."

Jamie couldn't help but hear Nippawanock's words vibrating in his mind. They stirred ideas and built identity. "The Native American could think himself superior to nothing," Uncle Nip said many times. "If anything, he is less than equal to his elder relatives of the animal, insect, bird, and plant nations. After all, who needs whom? Humans need them to survive. They do not need us.

"We need them for our food, clothing, and shelter, and to show us ways to live in peace. Do animals make weapons of war to slaughter each other?"

One day on the bus, Showanna Jones asked Jamie what his god, the Great Mystery, looked like. "I bet you can't even draw a picture of him," she said.

"How can you draw a picture of all things living together for all time?" Uncle Nip asked later when he heard the story. "No, Jamie, no Indian ever tried to picture what the Great Mystery looks like.

"We do, however, have a symbol that helps us to represent the Mystery — the Circle. It has no beginning and no end."

The circle seemed like a fitting symbol to Jamie. He would always remember Uncle Nip explaining, "Is not the earth round? And does she not move, spinning slowly, in a circle around the sun, which is also round? And are not the stars round, and do not the great galaxies of stars spin in great spirals? The trunks of trees, the eagle's eggs, even our bodies are round. Do not the seasons move in circles, and life too? Circles within circles.

"In a circle, all parts have equal importance. In any circle of people, if one person leaves, the circle is broken. It doesn't matter if that person is a small child or a huge football player. Without either one of them, the circle would not be complete. And that is how traditional-thinking Native Americans see all things— as part of the great Circle of Life.

"And where is the center of the circle of an endless universe? It is everywhere and within each of us, making us all relatives of equal value and importance.

"That's why," Uncle Nip continued, "Native Americans could not hunt for sport. A man should kill only what he needs in order to survive. That's why Indians could not have zoos where animals are imprisoned for human entertainment and amusement. That's why

Indians could not use animals for experiments. Animals have even more right to be here than we do. After all, kid, weren't they here first?"

Uncle Nip told Jamie that to the traditional Indian, everything is equal, and Jamie learned that many Indians even apologize to a plant if they have to take it for food, medicine, or lodging. The People understand their dependence on the animal and plant nations for their well-being.

One day, Uncle Nip asked Jamie to bring in a basket of kumquats from one of the fruit trees in the yard.

They were ripe and tasty, and Jamie couldn't help but feast on them. After all, there were so many. When he came into the house with a basket that was only half full, Nippawanock asked him where the rest were.

Again Jamie wondered how a nearly full-grown person, like himself, could act and feel so much like a little boy. "I guess I ate them all, Uncle," he replied, embarrassed. "I guess I didn't realize I did until now."

Uncle Nip shook his head at his nephew's gluttony, but he wouldn't let the moment escape without a lesson. "I want you to go back out there and thank the tree," he said firmly.

For some time Jamie stood silently by the tree that had provided his feast. At first, he felt silly. "Here I am," he thought, "in eighth grade, and I've got to talk to a tree." Then he said the words, "Thank you, brother." He felt a connection to the tree for having fed him. He knew that he and the tree were equal. He began to understand the Mystery. He was learning humility, in the Indian way.

CHAPTER 9

Even God Is Part of the Great Mystery

If today I had a young mind to direct, to start on the journey of life . . . I would for its welfare . . . set that child's feet in the path of my forefathers. I would raise him to be an Indian!

—from *Land of the Spotted Eagle,*
by Luther Standing Bear

Jamie was often asked if he believed in God. Did he go to some Indian church or something? Although he was learning from Uncle Nip the words he needed to explain these things, the questions still made him uncomfortable. "The Indian church is the earth and the sky," he'd say. That just brought laughter from some of the kids. Jamie was always reminded of how different he was. That's why he really hated those questions. Sometimes the questions were asked because a few kids were curious. Other times the questions were more like taunts.

"Do a rain dance!" That was Leroy's standard passing comment after he failed to make Jamie less than a whole person. He no longer hung around for Jamie's response."

"God exists for many people in the same way our gods exist for us," explained Uncle Nip. "Although they can't see their God, they believe that their prayers are heard. Likewise, our gods and the Great Mystery hear our prayers too.

"Our people believe that there are gods and other supernatural forces in nature that create things and make things happen, like the rain. We have great belief in the power of the Word too. We sing our chants to the mysterious and unseen. And we accompany them with the rhythms of music. Because we believe in the magic of the Word to make things happen, things do happen. Our prayers have magic. For many generations, traditional Indians have lived by and depended on these beliefs.

"You see," Nippawanock explained, "the People pray in some of the same ways as many other people. We don't pray to Jehovah or God or Brahma or Allah. We address Sakoiatisan, Kitche-Manitou, Taiowa, or Wakan-Tanka, depending on whether we are Iroquois, Ojibwa, Hopi, or Lakota, but we are always praying to the Maker and Container of All, the Great Mystery.

"And just as a Catholic believes in asking help of certain saints or angels who have special powers, many Indians ask their gods and spirits for help. Just as a Christian believes in Satan, the Devil, so do we have an evil being or spirit. But we believe that even what we call evil is a part of the Great Mystery. It is also a part of each of us."

Soon, Uncle Nip helped Jamie find a way not to let that evil control him. He taught Jamie about the Vision. Having a vision would one day make Jamie a man and give him direction and power in his life. These gifts he would use to help his people.

Nippawanock taught Jamie how to prepare for the prayer-fast. A prayer-fast is when a person stays alone for as long as four days, sometimes without eating or drinking anything. During this time, prayers are spoken to the Great Mystery. "A vision comes from your own juices," Uncle Nip explained. So, he encouraged his nephew not to eat or drink for a day, and sometimes even longer. Through this training, Jamie was preparing to go on a prayer-fast by himself and to seek a vision in this way.

Jamie learned that the People traditionally believe that the Great Mystery speaks to a person through the spirit of an animal or bird, insect, plant, or stone in a vision. Or perhaps a ghost might come. The Mystery might send something else that only the seeker would see and understand. If Jamie's heart was good, a vision would give him the direction he sought in life and the power to live it as a Native American. He learned much about visions from his Uncle Nip.

Jamie was not quite old enough to seek a vision through the prayer-fast. "You are preparing," Uncle Nip said. "When you are ready, you will go."

The vision would make Jamie a man. No one would ever be able to take it away. Not Mrs. Henshaw. Not missionaries. And certainly not Leroy Puckett. He would no longer become confused or angry when asked about the existence of God. "I believe in God, if you do," he was learning to say to those who asked. "Like all things, God is part of the Great Mystery."

CHAPTER 10

The Spirit Light

Happily I recover.
Happily my interior becomes cool.
Happily I go forth.
My interior feeling cool, may I walk.
No longer sore, may I walk.
Without pain, may I walk.
With lively feelings, may I walk.
As it used to be long ago, may I walk. . . .

> — from the Navaho "Beautyway"
> chant

▼▼▼

The years had flown by for Uncle Nip and Jamie. For Nip, it seemed like yesterday when he discovered a lost Indian boy wandering in a shopping mall, alone and hungry. He said that old age made remembering a funny

thing. "When you're old like me, you can remember what happened years ago so clearly," he explained, "but you can't remember what you had for breakfast."

For Jamie, it felt as if Uncle Nip had always been a part of his life. It was as if the boarding school and Mrs. Henshaw never really existed. They were just a distant memory of another lifetime. They were what he needed in order to find Uncle Nip. Uncle Nip was supposed to happen.

When Jamie graduated from high school, he received his diploma; he also earned a new name. In the backyard of Nip's house, Jamie's new name was introduced to the world. Uncle Nip raised his pipe high while he faced each of the Four Directions and called out the name. He asked the powers of the world to know the name and to welcome his nephew. He raised the pipe to the sky and lowered it to the earth. He called out the name to the plant and animal nations. He spoke the name to the moon, the sun, and the stars. Then he addressed the Great Mystery. Each time he said the name — One Who Finds the Path.

When their ceremony was complete, Uncle Nip smiled proudly at his nephew. Jamie smiled back. The spirit light sparkled brightly in his black eyes.

PART II

Medicine Man

▼▼▼

CHAPTER 1

It Wasn't Easy Holding On

▲▲▲

When my sister started [school], the teacher cut her hair, burned all her clothes, and gave her a new outfit and a new name, Nellie. . . . Although my brother was two years older than me, he had managed to keep out of school, but he had to be careful not to be seen by Whites. When he finally did enter the day school at New Oraibi, they cut his hair, burned his clothes, and named him Ira."

— from *Sun Chief, The Autobiography of a Hopi Indian*, by Don C. Talayesva

▼▼▼

I t's not every day an American Indian medicine man comes to school. In fact, it was the first time that anything like that had ever happened at Pine Bay Elementary. The whole school was excited. Signs were posted everywhere: "Tom Peek, American Indian Medicine Man." Lots of kids were curious. It showed by the way they became unusually quiet when our principal talked about Mr. Peek's arrival over the PA during morning announcements. The place seemed to vibrate all week from anticipation.

When the teachers found out where Mr. Peek would be speaking, they all tried to get their classes to go. This meant that most of the school population would cram into a few classrooms that day. Even office workers and custodians were planning to slip in to listen. Everyone seemed to make arrangements for the visit. The occasion was that special.

Most of the classes had just finished a Thanksgiving unit on Indians. Still, we didn't know what to expect. Some teachers talked about Indians in class. They did not want anyone to make fun of the medicine man because he was "different."

I wasn't sure, but I figured Mr. Peek would bring a drum and rattle. I'd seen such things on television. I remembered pictures of a medicine man I had seen in a book on Indians back in third or fourth grade. I wondered if he was going to wear some kind of headdress with horns and feathers and such. You'd think that being Indian would have helped to prepare me.

But, the truth be known, my father split when I was young. He went to Los Angeles to find work and never came back. Mom says it was because he had a problem with drinking. Anyway, he was stabbed outside some bar and died shortly after. He was forty-four. My social studies teacher later told me that the average life span of an American Indian man is forty-four years. I guess he died when an Indian man was expected to die.

My mom, on the other hand, stayed with me. She was proud of my Indian spirit, and she showed it by naming me "Red Elk." She also said she didn't know much about Indian things. After her folks died when she was thirteen, she was sent to an orphanage. When her folks were young, they had been taken by government agents to a boarding school. They were taught to be ashamed of their Indian heritage. The purpose of such schools was to give Indians an education. The schools believed that the best way to do it was for the kids to stop being Indians.

Back then, my mom says, being an Indian was not something you bragged about. You know how today you hear people say that they're part Indian? In those days you didn't say that. Being Indian could cause you lots of pain. The white man was trying hard to wash the Indian out of the People and the country back then. So, my mom's parents never made a point of teaching her the old Indian ways. They said the old ways wouldn't help in this white man's world.

When the government was taking over her parents' reservation, there were many different denominations of missionaries there. They were trying to outdo each other to save the souls of Indians. The competition became fierce. The government finally stepped in to help. What they did was to have the People form lines. Then the government agent divided them up, saying this line is Baptist, this one's Catholic, this one's Episcopal. He did it until every Indian on my mom's reservation belonged to a church.

On a lot of reservations, Indians were forbidden to practice the old ceremonies. Sometimes, Mom said, their homes were broken into and their religious things were taken. Church on Sunday was often the only place where Indians were allowed to gather.

The kids were sent away to boarding school. They got to come home during the Christmas holidays, so naturally they grew to like Christmas a lot. The Christmas tradition of giving presents went along with the People well, since things like "give-aways" were already a part of Native American customs. Of course, most of the People were too poor to buy presents, so the churches handed them out to the kids. Mom says they made lots of converts among the kids this way — even if just for the Christmas holidays.

After the holidays, though, those Indian children were on the train or the big yellow bus once again, headed back to boarding school. If there were any holdouts or kids who came of school age during the year, they went along too and were welcomed in much the same way as the others before them.

The first thing the teachers did in many of those boarding schools was to cut off the hair of the Indian boys and girls. My mom said that apparently hair had something to do with expressing your identity. She said

an elder once told her that sometimes you can tell the wisdom of a man by the length of his braids. She said that in some tribes, cutting hair was a sign that someone you loved had just died. So, by cutting off the children's hair, those boarding-school teachers were cutting off the kids' ties to the past.

The boarding schools wanted those boys and girls to look and act like the white man's idea of how people should look and act. That's what my mom said. The Indian kids were forced to wear uniforms. The Navaho girls' pretty turquoise jewelry, the Apache boys' bandannas, the Seminole kids' colorful jackets and dresses, and the Ojibwa children's beaded flowers were all replaced by gray dresses or pants and white shirts and ties.

The teachers also felt the need to strongly discourage the children from wanting to be Indians. The Indian kids were forbidden to speak their native languages. That's why Mom never learned to speak hers.

I began to wonder how other kids would feel if the Chinese, or any other people, came and conquered this country and snatched kids from their parents, sending them far away to school to live. There, the only language they could speak would be Chinese. If they were caught speaking English, they would be either severely punished or beaten.

That's not all the government did, my mom says. They forbade the children to pray the way they were used to. Even though they didn't have the drums to accompany their words, some of the children still knew the songs, but the songs were also forbidden. They wouldn't let the

People believe the ancient ways taught by their parents and elders. Instead, Indians were taught the Bible and how to be Christians and to sing "Amazing Grace." Some of our people accepted these new beliefs, but others couldn't.

If the children became sick at school, they went to a white doctor for treatment. Often he would prescribe some pill or liquid. He never prescribed the Indian herbal teas to drink or the medicine roots to chew. And too often the white doctor couldn't help.

Most of the medical doctors didn't realize that the children's illnesses came from imbalance in their lives. A new diet, new ways to pray, a new language, the separation from their families, and uncomfortable uniforms in place of their native dress all were causes of stress on those kids. The stress created an imbalance in them — mentally, physically, and spiritually. It's no wonder they got sick.

The medicine men were not there. But even at home, they were usually forbidden to practice their healing rituals. In short, the kids were denied any way other than the white man's.

Mom says that her mom used to talk about some of those Indian kids and how tough they were about resisting the changes. In a way, she said, in their kid minds, those children seemed determined not to lose their Indian identities. The way her mother talked about them, it was as if she was ashamed that she wasn't tough too.

Some spoke their native languages when they figured they couldn't get caught. Others ran away to hide out with elders and/or the medicine people, who were hiding out themselves.

The medicine men couldn't help the children who were away at boarding school. They did, however, try to keep the old ways alive. Secretly they performed healing ceremonies and other rituals. They did this at great risk.

A few kids couldn't handle the boarding schools at all. Some of them died while trying to run away. My grandmother used to cry over one little ten-year-old friend who died in the snow, frozen to death, trying to get away. There were other children who actually killed themselves, she said.

My mom and grandmother told me all these things. This made having a medicine man come to Pine Bay more special for me. No, I thought to myself, I didn't know much about being Indian. But Mom did name me Red Elk.

CHAPTER 2

Medicine and Sweat Lodges

▲▲▲

**"You sit there quietly in the dark. . . . You
close your eyes, listen to the hiss of the icy
water on the heated stones, listen to what
they have to tell you. . . . This inipi [sweat
lodge] is our little church."**

—from *Lame Deer, Seeker of Visions*,
by John Fire and Richard Erdoes

▼▼▼

Tom Peek's braided white hair told me that those
boarding-school teachers may have forgotten that
hair grows back. Mr. Peek greeted us in an Indian language. I figured he must have been one of those kids
who spoke "Indian" when the teachers weren't around.

He carried a bundle and a pipe. I'd say the missionaries hadn't been too successful at "saving" Mr. Peek. These were among the religious articles many Indians were not allowed to keep.

I don't know what it was, but something happened to all of us when he came into our packed classroom. We actually listened. Even though he was different-looking, we thought he was cool. Maybe we were just happy that people like him really do still exist. Maybe he made us all feel a lot freer than we ever had before.

He glanced at us sitting in a crowded circle and smiled. We could see right off that we pleased him. For one thing, we all got real quiet. Usually, when guest speakers came, the teachers had to stand and give us evil stares to make us not talk or goof around. But when Tom Peek started to speak, there wasn't a sound. The teachers even sat among the kids, sort of like they were kids too.

He told us in plain English that there are more than 400 different kinds of Indian medicine used to keep us healthy today. The white man hasn't discovered one new medicine from this land that the Indian didn't already know about. From the common aspirin to what doctors call modern "miracle drugs," Native Americans were very much in tune with maintaining good health. They knew how to regain it when they were wounded or ill.

He said that one Indian medicine alone is responsible for saving the lives of thousands of American soldiers in the Pacific during World War II. Some historians believe that if it weren't for the Native American drug called quinine, the United States might have lost the war in that part of the world. Quinine cures malaria, a disease infecting thousands of soldiers.

"Nobody likes being sick or in pain," Mr. Peek explained. "That's why Indian cures and pain relievers became so popular among the early settlers in the nineteenth century. Places were named 'Medicine Lake' or 'Medicine Bow,' even 'Medicine Gap' and 'Medicine Gulch.' They all had a connection to Indian medicine. Then came Buffalo Bill and His Wild West Show! Hollywood soon followed. Movies showed the Indian as an enemy and a fierce warrior. The Indian as healer was forgotten."

"Yes," he said, "Native Americans were a very healthy race. There were few major diseases in this hemisphere until the white man came. One reason was the simple practice of bathing. Indians bathed at least once a day, even if it meant cutting a hole in the ice on a winter morning. A day without a bath was considered unhealthy. I still get angry watching movies about Indians. They always seem dirty or are called dirty savages."

He explained that Indians had different kinds of baths. One was the bath simply to cleanse the body on the outside. It could be done once in the morning and once in the evening in a river, creek, lake, or pond. But another had to do with cleansing the body from the inside. This type of bath took place in a sweat lodge. The purpose of this internal bathing was ceremonial.

Mr. Peek described the sweat lodge that stood in his backyard. He and a good friend built it using red willow. They made it four feet high and eight feet in diameter, covering it with blankets, sleeping bags, and canvas. Then they put red-hot stones, called "grandfathers," on the ground in the center. Working together, the two of them established a sort of Indian brotherhood, even though they were not blood-related.

Mr. Peek said that he knows of no Indian nation without the tradition of sweat lodges. Although the size of sweat lodges varied from man to man and tribe to tribe, most had several things in common. One was their shape. Every sweat lodge he had ever seen or read about was built in a circle that resembles a beehive. In the old days, most Indians used buffalo hides or other local materials to cover the lodge. After the lodge is covered, the red-hot grandfather stones are placed in its center in a sacred manner. The Indian always greets each stone as he enters. Mr. Peek said that he believes everything is alive, including rocks. They have helped him very much in his life, so he treats them with great respect.

When entering a sweat lodge, people hunch down on all fours. Inside, they find a place to sit cross legged, or they just squat in a circle around the stones. Then the pipe is passed around, allowing each person to address and thank the Great Mystery. Next, the medicine man pours cold water on the red-hot stones. The grandfathers crackle and hiss and release more heat than you think your body can stand. You begin to sweat all the poisons and toxins from your body. As you sweat, the medicine man may sing sacred songs, and the People, huddled close to Mother Earth, begin to pray. Then, just when you think you can not stand any more heat, the medicine man

fans you with eagle feathers, which makes the lodge even hotter!

People are usually naked inside the sweat lodge. It is like returning to the womb — it is the womb of Mother Earth. Indians never used to have shame for the body. Shame was taught by the missionaries. "Nowadays," Mr. Peek said, "it's better that women sometimes have their own sweat ceremonies, if that makes them feel more comfortable."

When the ceremony is over, coming out of the sweat lodge is like being "born again" in an Indian way. Mr. Peek laughed, saying, "You aren't born with clothes on, or jewelry, for that matter, so you can understand the meaning of nakedness." The best thing to do right after you come out, with the steam still rising from your skin, is to head for the nearest body of cold water and jump in. "That's feeling alive!" he said.

Mr. Peek told us that modern scientists have verified that this method of bathing can help to prevent diseases such as cancer. It also helps to cure arthritis and rheumatism. But it does something even more: It heals your mind and your heart. It brings balance back into the lives of the People.

The Indians used another bath for healing, soaking in the many hot springs in our land. This type of bathing went on for long periods of time. It helped to relieve the tension of everyday life. The warm, moving waters relax the muscles, open the pores, and stimulate healing.

Mr. Peek told how some people who want to make money have, unfortunately, taken over most of the places where mineral springs are, and now they charge admission for their use. In one such place in Florida, only wealthy people can use the warm springs, because they put a wall around them and called it a "club." Indians can no longer use the springs in that peaceful old way. It's ironic that the white man once considered these bathing practices to be savage and unhealthy, but now they control them and charge money for their use.

The Spanish banned this type of bathing, yet, it was the American Indian who was clean and disease-free. Once these practices were banned and new European diseases were introduced here, Native Americans died by the tens of thousands. Whole nations became extinct!

Mr. Peek said that some historians estimate that 90 percent of the Native American population died from European diseases in the first 100 years of their occupation of the North and South American continents. Epidemics of measles, whooping cough, and mumps swept through Indian villages and wiped them out. In the white man's town, though, people just got pretty sick; they didn't often die. The reason is simple. It took generations for the white man to build up a tolerance to these diseases, so when a measles epidemic spread through an average town, it didn't kill everyone. But it sure did kill within the Native American communities, and it still does! Recently, whole tribes of Indians who live in the rain forests of South America have been exterminated by treatable diseases such as measles and mumps.

Mr. Peek also said that alcohol is a disease. Benjamin Franklin thought that with the use of alcohol the American Indian could be "extirpated [this was the word

Franklin used] in order to make room for the cultivators of the earth." Ben Franklin figured that by the use of rum (alcohol), the Indians could be wiped out by those, like him, who were cultivating somebody else's land. That's probably what killed my father as much as the knife of some coward, I thought. I understood what Mr. Peek and Ben Franklin said about alcohol.

Smallpox also devastated the Native American population. Few people realize that American Indians were the first people to have germ warfare used against them, first by Lord Jeffrey Amherst of the British, then by the Americans, who, in 1763, issued gifts to the People — smallpox-infested blankets that were taken from infected and dying soldiers at Fort Pitt.

One kid asked why Indians needed medicine if they had no diseases before the white man came.

Mr. Peek said that Indians got aches and pains just like we do today. They also got wounds from battle or from hunting. And there are natural illnesses that come with living close to nature, such as a severe reaction to a snakebite or a case of poison ivy. But nature has remedies. The medicine people of each tribe and nation sought, throughout their lives, to find ways to help their people.

Other kinds of sickness — sickness of the mind and of the heart — can create an imbalance in a person's life, and he or she will get sick as a result. Some Hopi and Cherokee medicine people used crystals to detect illness in a person. With these sacred objects, they would examine the body's several centers to find the one out of balance. Many Native people believe that illness can be caused by another person or by something outside the body which affects one of the centers. The medicine man or woman has to find the imbalance and cure it.

When he said "woman," we all blinked. "You mean a woman could be a medicine man too?" one kid asked.

Mr. Peek chuckled. "Sure," he said, still smiling. "In a way, she could, but she didn't have to become a man in order to know how to heal.

"As a matter of fact," he said, "there really wasn't any such person as a medicine man — not in the way you grew up thinking. No one man was the cure for all the tribe. No one medicine man was endowed with all the knowledge for healing wounds, fixing broken bones, doctoring sick stomachs, and delivering babies. No one person could interpret visions and dreams, teach stories, predict the weather, and change the weather to rain or sunshine, depending on the need. No one medicine man could help those folks who were hurting in their minds or hearts and conduct the ceremonies for naming, marriage, and death. No one person could heal, organize the feasts and festivals of each moon and of the planting and harvesting times, and be the one to announce the arrivals of the winter and summer solstices and the days of the spring or autumn equinox.

"He would be one busy man!" Mr. Peek gasped.

CHAPTER 3

Indian Medicine, Music, and Magic

"Do you see? There, far off into the darkness, something happened. Do you see? Far, far away in the nothingness something happened. There was a voice, a sound, a word — and everything began."

— from *House Made of Dawn,*
by N. Scott Momaday

▼▼▼

*M*edicine man. How can this term be used for all the different men and women with gifts to help heal the People? "More than likely," Mr. Peek said, "*medicine man* was not a term Native people used. It didn't really work for them."

I think Mr. Peek was saying that he did not consider himself to be a medicine man. Some of the teachers began to squirm in their undersized student desks — and the kids too. After all, his visit had been advertised around school as "Tom Peek, American Indian Medicine Man, Comes to Pine Bay Elementary." Every poster hanging in every corridor read "Indian Medicine Man."

"If you want to call me a medicine man, go ahead," he said, "though you might think differently after I'm done speaking to you today." Mr. Peek listed other terms for medicine man that we use today: doctor, healer, shaman, sorcerer, and witchdoctor. Most folks, though, have accepted the title "medicine man."

He said that no one man or woman can cure even a fraction of all the different types of sickness. "My grandmother knew plants better than anyone I've ever known. If a person went to her and needed medicine for a bad stomach or something to help fight infection, she could take a walk in the woods and find a medicine to heal the ailment. She never took a thing from nature without either saying thanks and apologizing to the plant she needed or leaving an offering of tobacco."

You should know some things about asking someone like his grandmother for help, he said. For one thing, the person who needs such services usually brings tobacco or a special feather or some other gift of the heart to her. One man, knowing her husband had died, brought her a winter month's supply of venison. She needed the food. He needed a cure for infection. Another man brought her heating oil for a month in return for her trying to help his

sick daughter who had severe stomach cramps. These men brought their gifts before they asked for cures. They had respect for and faith in the healer's prayers and songs. They also had respect for the herbs of Mother Earth!

"None of these medicine people," our guest speaker emphasized, "practiced their skills for money. They wanted only to help their people. By bringing them something sacred or useful or just special in some way, you make a commitment to use what they give you to heal yourself."

Mr. Peek explained that some healing requires a special ceremony. "For instance, the Navaho medicine man creates a sand painting to evoke the healing powers. In many of these ceremonies, an instrument, such as a rattle or gourd or water drum, is used to accompany the songs. These healing songs are special songs. They are handed down from generation to generation, or they are taught to the medicine man in his dreams and visions. They are sacred. Together the ceremonies and songs work magic — and the magic is strong!

"Native Americans have always had great respect for and belief in the Power of the Word. In every creation account of the People, the Word is connected to the Great Mystery. In some accounts the Word came first, causing the creative process to unfold. Sometimes the Word came shortly afterwards. The Word is always directly linked to the Great Mystery. The Word can help plants to grow; it can cause medicine to work. The Word allows a Native American to speak to and be heard by the First Cause of All."

Mr. Peek said that one of the most accepted scientific theories about the origin of the universe is called the "big bang." This theory asserts that at one time all matter in the universe was one. Then there was a tremendous explosion, and everything began; this was the "big bang." In some ways, he explained, this is similar to what Native Americans believe, but to them, the creation is not just a big bang but something that is incredibly sacred. The Zuni, for instance, describe the Beginning of Newness when "Awonawilona [the Maker and Container of All] . . . thought outward into space. . . ." The opening of this creation account, he said, shows how sound and the Word are linked to the Creation itself.

I didn't know that back in the days when Indians spoke in their native languages, there were no swear words, because Indians understood the sacred relationship between speaking, creating and healing. An Indian might have growled like a wolf at you if he were angry enough, but he couldn't swear — at least not in his Native language. It was only when Indians went to boarding schools and learned English that they learned how to swear. Unfortunately, Indians also learned how to abuse language by saying things they didn't mean, or by using words to get what they wanted, or even by spreading gossip.

All the time today we hear people shout "Jeeezus Christ!" or "Goddamnit!" Because of the sacred connection to the Great Mystery, a Native American could have never used the Word in that way. Mr. Peek paused. "How can your prayers have power if you abuse the Word?

How can you lie, swear, and abuse the name of your God and expect your prayers to have power?" He shook his head.

Painting intricate and sacred symbols on the sands of Mother Earth or singing sacred songs requires a flawless ceremony. To make a mistake in beating the drum or to stammer over the words ruins the healing process.

"You see," Mr. Peek said, "when you sing and beat out a rhythm on the drum, you're making vibrations that can cause things to happen. We all know that sound has vibration. Ever experienced a sonic boom or a clap of thunder over your house?" Everyone nodded.

By singing a sacred song over and over and believing in its power, you can actually cause something to happen. It's called *incantation*. Breaking the rhythm means that the song loses its flowing connection to the healing powers of the Great Mystery. It's sort of like when you're trying to draw a straight line and someone bumps your arm. The line is no longer straight.

"Another thing you should know," he said, "has to do with belief. Belief is half the cure. Without belief in the medicine or its link to the Indian's belief in nature and the Creation, my grandmother couldn't have fixed any of the people who came to her for help. By believing in the medicine and in the power of the Word, the People had to assume the rest of the responsibility for healing themselves."

Mr. Peek paused, looked at me, and smiled. I doubt if anyone else saw it, but I sure did. His smile and his eyes penetrated me. He seemed young for being so old, and gentle for being so strong.

"Just like you," he explained, "I've been to the doctor's office for some ailment I needed help to cure and to the dentist's office to get my teeth fixed; they did what they knew how to do, but I had to help heal myself."

He told us about the Indians of Mexico who were the first people to use gold and silver fillings in their teeth. Other Indians could perform surgery, as did the Incas of the Andes in ancient times.

Archaeologists have uncovered skulls several centuries old with rather large holes in them. Scientists have found evidence that the Native Americans had medicine men who were actually surgeons — brain surgeons!

The skulls revealed that head wounds sustained in battle, or by some other cause, could be treated by drilling into the skull of the injured person. The drilling relieved dangerous and life-threatening pressure on the brain. The Indian surgeons, particularly the Aztecs, used obsidian tools for such a task. These early scalpels were made so thin that they barely left a scar. Today, he said, incisions made with steel scalpels are not as precise; only incisions made by laser beams can compare.

Some skulls found by these archaeologists had as many as five holes in them, each showing that the healing process was completed. The injured person went on to live a longer life.

I began to wonder what was done to the people who went through surgery. Were they put to sleep or hypnotized or something? Mr. Peek explained that Indians had drugs and pain killers for just such purposes. Natural ones were provided by the tree and plant nations.

Although the chemicals of certain plants mixed together will kill a person, it's amazing that the Indian medicine people were able to mix plants together and come up with helpful medicines without there being any recorded deaths. They learned this chemistry through dreaming and vision-seeking. In the dream or vision a medicine person was shown how to use certain herbs to help the People.

Mr. Peek made a point of saying that Native Americans, with all their knowledge of herbs, medicines, and drugs, never had a drug-abuse problem. Today, some people become hopelessly addicted to drugs, and they even steal or kill to satisfy their addiction.

Cocaine is an example of such a drug. In its natural leafy form (coca), it was used by Native Americans in South America for a variety of reasons. They didn't need laws to guard their citizens from abusers, and they created sharing, peaceful societies. One recent television documentary reported that the Inca Indians saw how crazed the Spanish became over cocaine. An Inca leader remarked that the white man's abuse would one day be his destruction.

Tobacco, another drug, was highly regarded by Native Americans. Not only was it used for medicinal purposes, but when it was smoked, it was used in a special, often religious, manner.

The "New World" Europeans perverted the use of these drugs. They either forbade Indians to use them or, as in the case of the coca leaves, they forced Indians to eat them in order to become better slaves. The coca leaves helped them to work longer hours. They needed less oxygen in the mines. They needed less to eat. Indians died by the thousands under such conditions. Rather than become enslaved, some Native Americans willed themselves to die.

The drugs of the coca and tobacco leaves were also regarded as money by the white man. Today we can see the result of this attitude everywhere. In some places it's not safe to walk at night for fear of being mugged or murdered for money by a cocaine addict. Cigarette smoking is a killer that causes horrible cancer deaths and heart disease, yet it is linked to big money-making tobacco farms and a multibillion-dollar industry.

One kid asked if that stuff about singing during a healing ceremony and eating plants from the woods ever worked for white people. Our guest speaker told us about a Spaniard named Cabeza de Vaca. He was an explorer during the sixteenth century who kept journals of his explorations and meetings with the Indians.

During one excursion, De Vaca was shipwrecked in Florida. He described how the Native Americans found him on the shore. They cried at the horrible state he and his men were in, nearly starved to death. They took him and his surviving crew into their village as brothers.

In his journal, De Vaca wrote that there were Christians living on the island who told him not to go to the Indian village. "The savages will sacrifice you!" they warned.

De Vaca and his crew were not "sacrificed." In fact, they were well-fed and cared for by those "savages." The Indians doctored them with medical practices unknown to the Europeans. Mending wounds by cauterizing them was totally new to the Spanish, as were the other Indian remedies and medicines that saved those explorers' lives. In return, however, the Indians required their guests, once they were well enough, to work or contribute in some other way to the village. "No Indian nation cared for freeloaders," Mr. Peek said.

He added that each day it appears we're learning more and more about what the Indians have already known or used to know and about how little modern medicine really knows. He considers himself to be living proof that the Indian way can work, even in today's modern technological world. "So are all of you in this room living proof of the Indian way," he said.

"You can believe the Earth is your mother or not. You can believe you're related to all things or not. But we're all healthy due to Indian foods, medicines, and practices. But now we eat our corn and our beans from cans and buy our fries at McDonald's. We take our aspirin when we have a headache and get stitches when we're cut. In much the same way, the Native Americans of long ago did the same things.

"I'm here today because of my Indian beliefs," Mr. Peek proudly acknowledged. I decided right then to learn all I could of the Indian ways. I wanted to be like him. I figured that's why he smiled at me. Maybe it was one reason he came to Pine Bay Elementary that day.

CHAPTER 4

The Rain Forest

Far as man can see,
Comes the rain,
Comes the rain with me. . . .

Over the corn,
Over the corn, tall corn,
Comes the rain,
Comes the rain with me. . . .

Far as man can see,
Comes the rain,
Comes the rain with me.

> —from the Navaho "Song
> of the Rain" Chant

▼▼▼

Mr. Peek's eyes became watery and his voice raspy when he talked about the destruction of the land for human development. He was especially bewildered at the destruction of the rain forests for money.

"Thinking we can destroy the rain forests and still keep this world habitable is like thinking there can be a winner in a nuclear war. It's just plain stupidity!" he said.

He described the rain forests as natural gardens where undiscovered plants live that might one day cure every disease in the world — even cancer and AIDS. He said that civilized man knows only a small fraction of the medicinal plants that dwell there.

I learned that to destroy the rain forests may be our final act against Mother Earth. The Native people who are protecting the rain forests in this hemisphere are the few Native American tribes and nations that have somehow survived there — and survival for them has been hard. Some South American countries did not pass laws against killing an Indian until the latter part of the twentieth century. The missionaries, eager to spread the news of Christianity to these people, infected the natives with deadly diseases. Government helicopter gunships have, at times, sprayed entire Indian villages with gunfire in order to make them leave the land. Many innocent people were killed, and others were, and still are, chased deeper into the jungle, away from their homes.

The Indian has always been the protector of this land, and so we have also been in the way of this thing called "civilization." When killing Indians was no longer acceptable in this country, the white man took us to boarding schools. That's what happened to my mom's parents. They decided to try to de-Indianize us and to get us out of the way by making us ashamed and keeping us ignorant of the great contributions of our ancestors.

What really got to me that day was how much this medicine man believed in what he was saying and how much he knew. When he talked about water and the rain forests, I felt like standing up and yelling "STOP RUINING OUR WORLD!" as loud as I could to all the governments responsible for the destruction — and I know there are many. But, instead, I listened as he spoke with watery eyes about how pure water is medicinal. Water is the life-blood of the Earth. By polluting our rivers, lakes, and streams, we are polluting the very body of Mother Earth. It's like injecting into our veins and arteries chemicals that eventually will travel to our hearts and kill us.

Treating Mother Earth so senselessly will jeopardize our survival. Even I could understand this, and I never considered myself a great student. How could the people in power in this world not be as smart as I am? How could they accept the destruction of the rain forests and the native people? In those forests of Central and South America, as in just about any forest in North America, including Alaska, the medicines of the world are growing. There live the medicine men and women who know how to use them. The very air we breathe comes from plants and trees. And our rain water — my gosh, that's what we need to live!

CHAPTER 5

Medicine and Masks

▲▲▲

In the summer Katchinas with great heads and fine clothes came into the plaza and danced. They almost never spoke, but sang a great deal. An old man, called the Father of the Katchinas . . . asked them to go home at sunset and send us rain. . . . Everybody knew they were spirit gods.

— from *Sun Chief, The Autobiography of a Hopi Indian*, by Don C. Talayesva

▼▼▼

"Medicine to the Native American," Mr. Peek said, "is not just something we drink in the form of teas or swallow in tablets. Medicine can be in a stone or a feather or just about anything you believe has power. Either through a dream or vision, or through someone's gift, an object can have special spiritual qualities. It can even be something you wear for protection, as the great Sioux leader Crazy Horse did."

Mr. Peek explained that Crazy Horse wore a small round stone behind his ear and a sparrow hawk's feather tied to his hair when he went into combat with United States troops. He wore the stone to protect himself from bullets. Crazy Horse would charge into the thick of battle as bullets whizzed past him. He believed that the stone and feather gave him power. They must have, for Crazy Horse was never shot by a soldier.

Mr. Peek picked up his bundle. It was his medicine bundle. In it were special things that only he knew. He said that he hoped every Indian had one, and he glanced at me as he spoke.

Once he was staying on one of the Iroquois reservations in the state of New York. There was a great deal of concern among the traditional people, especially the elders. The schools and the surrounding white community were gearing up for Halloween. One of the elementary schools was planning a Halloween party. All the kids were expected to come wearing costumes. Sounds like fun for most of us, and to some of the Iroquois kids too, no doubt.

But there was a problem — a big problem — for a people trying to retain their cultural and spiritual identity in their native land. Most Halloween costumes come with masks. Masks for these Iroquois, as well most other traditional Native Americans, are considered sacred — or at least very important. In most tribes, only certain people wear them.

The Iroquois man takes his mask from a living tree, carving the section and removing it while the tree still stands. The man sees in such a tree the spirit form of the mask he will carve. Such a mask can have great power when the man uses it to heal a sick person or drive away evil influences.

One such mask is in the form of a "False Face." It has a distorted, magical appearance. Although the appearance of these masks may seem strange, they are not evil. In fact, when used by the False Face Society, they can cure illnesses and drive away evil influences. Their healing qualities are available for the good of the People, but the face of the mask remains forever deformed.

The Onondaga elders of the Iroquois Confederacy once said, "Isn't it bad enough the pumpkins, a source of food and vitality to our people for countless generations, are so abused on this day called Halloween? And now we are to allow our children to wear masks? Any one of our people who wears a mask must take on the qualities and characteristics of the spirit being whose image is carved in the wood.... How can this power work if we allow our children to abuse it, solely in the name of Halloween fun? We can't."

Similar feelings are expressed across the country. During the ceremonies of the Hopi Indians, masked dancers called Katchinas move throughout the village, some bringing gifts, some bringing laughter, some looking for disobedient children. Each Katchina represents and becomes the spirit image of a spirit being — one who will bring rain, help corn to grow, or help the People to stay whole.

Medicine, like all things, tends to have both a good and a bad side, Mr. Peek emphasized. There are people who know this medicine power and who use it to hurt others. Originally, the medicine societies, like the Ojibwa Indians' Midé Society, were made up of only those people of good heart who would use medicine to do good; as time passed, that changed.

Even now there are traditional Navaho medicine people, who use sand paintings for healing, who are concerned that these sacred designs will be copied and sold as works of art. Although the paintings are created with incredible precision and beauty, they are not preserved. Because of these healers' respect for the painting, the painting is destroyed after each ceremony. In this way, the Navaho feel that the power is not abused. These healers believe that selling sand paintings at curio shops and art stores hurts the power of the ceremony and the sand paintings.

Others argue that the paintings offered for sale are not sacred. Either they do not have the secret symbols used in the ceremony, or they are not the complete paintings used in the ceremony. In any case, it is a heated and growing controversy.

Mr. Peek said that there is also great medicine in knowledge. It helps us all to grow in understanding. Understanding destroys hatred, violence, and confusion. "Always try to understand the ways of others, including animals, plants, and insects; respect those ways, so that we may come to know ourselves better."

We were all sad when Tom Peek left us that day. For some time after his visit, things were not quite the same at Pine Bay Elementary. There wasn't any pushing and shoving in the lunch line. There were no fights in the school yard, and the bathrooms no longer smelled of cigarette smoke. Teachers didn't have to yell; students didn't shout. Our principal had each class plant a tree for Arbor Day. For the rest of the year, our school was a quieter, more friendly place. I wonder if Tom Peek ever knew the impact he had on our lives. I think he did. That was his medicine.

ABOUT THE AUTHOR

Noted author and lecturer Gabriel Horn was given the name "White Deer of Autumn" by his uncles, Meta–comet and Nippawanock, and by Princess Red Wing of the Narragansett tribe, Wampanoag nation. He has taught in reservation schools, American Indian Movement (AIM) survival schools, public schools, and junior colleges. He helped develop the curriculum and was head teacher at the Red School House in St. Paul, Minnesota. He was cultural arts director of the Minneapolis American Indian Center from 1980 to 1982 and helped to establish the Minneapolis American Indian Art Gallery and the Living Traditions Museum. For his work in Indian rights, Gabriel Horn was nominated for the Human Rights Award in the state of Minnesota.

Gabriel Horn has a master's degree in English and currently devotes his time to lecturing, teaching, and writing. He is a teacher in Florida as well as a member of the National Committee on American Indian History and an advisor to the Native American national newspaper, *Indigenous Thought.* He lives on the Florida coast with his wife, Simone, an Ojibway, close to Mother Earth and the natural world that is so precious to him.

ABOUT THE ILLUSTRATOR

Shonto Begay is a Native American artist who specializes in multicultural illustrations. His other works include *The Mud Pony,* a Native American story, and *Lluvia,* a Hispanic children's book. He lives in Kayenta, Arizona, with his family. His illustrations for *Native People, Native Ways* accurately detail the traditional dress, architecture, and art of the many Native tribes in the various regions of the Americas throughout history.

ACKNOWLEDGMENTS

The "Native People, Native Ways" series would not have been accomplished without the support and assistance of my wife, Simone, and the sacrifices made by my loving children: Ihasha, Calusa, and Carises. Without Jay Johnson's belief in my work and Paige Graham's ability to work with draft after draft of each manuscript, and without Paige's constant reminders for me to listen to the ghost voices, these books would not reflect the quality that they have. I'm also grateful to the publishers of Beyond Words, Cynthia Black and Richard Cohn, who recognized the quality of the series and the needs that the books can help fulfill. Their proofreader, Marvin Moore, and Native American curriculum specialist, Chris Landon, fine-tuned the books in such a way as to make us all proud. And to Fred Brady and the other elders who sent their prayers into the Mystery that these books would become a reality for our children and grandchildren, I give my deepest gratitude. I would also like to thank my friend and agent, Sandra Martin, who continues to encourage me to write. I'm grateful to Shonto Begay for his spark of creativity that will help children to see Native people in a Native way. And lastly, I wish to acknowledge all the elders who took the time to teach me, and all the writers whose spirit enabled them to share what they too have learned from the Native People and Native Ways of this land.

Acknowledgment is gratefully made to the following authors and publishers who have granted permission to use selected quotations from their publications:

Eastman, Charles. *The Soul of the Indian.* Lincoln, Nebraska: University of Nebraska Press, 1980.

Mitchell, Black House Emerson. *Miracle Hill.* Norman, Oklahoma: University of Oklahoma Press, 1968.

Momaday, N. Scott. *House Made of Dawn.* New York: Harper & Row, 1989.

Sanders, Walter E. and Peaks, Walter W. *Literature of the American Indian.* Beverly Hills, California: Glencoe Press, 1973.

Talayesva, Don C. *Sun Chief, Autobiography of a Hopi Indian.* New Haven, Connecticut: Yale University Press, 1978.

Other Native American Children's Books from Beyond Words Publishing, Inc.

THE NATIVE AMERICAN BOOK OF KNOWLEDGE
Author: White Deer of Autumn
Illustrator: Shonto Begay
96 pages, $4.95 softbound, ages 10-12

Investigates the fascinating and controversial origins of the People, based on tales from various tribes, scientific evidence, and archaeological finds. Discusses several key figures in the Americas, including Deganawida, Hyonwatha, and others who have had a mystical and spiritual impact on the Native people.

THE NATIVE AMERICAN BOOK OF LIFE
Author: White Deer of Autumn
Illustrator: Shonto Begay
96 pages, $4.95 softbound, ages 10-12

Speaks of the great importance of children in the Native way of life; about their pastimes, how they are named, initiated into everyday society, taught, disciplined, and cared for. A fictional, magical story about children visiting a Native museum and learning about the many practices relating to food and the People: food growing and gathering practices, feasting traditions, and food contributions.

THE NATIVE AMERICAN BOOK OF CHANGE
Author: White Deer of Autumn
Illustrator: Shonto Begay
96 pages, $4.95 softbound, ages 10-12

Common stereotypes of Native Americans are explored and debunked, while passing on our personal "shields" — positive points of view that tell ourselves and others who and what we are — is encouraged. An important look back in time that focuses on the People's interaction with whites: The conquests of the Toltec, Aztec, Mayan, and North American tribes are covered.

CEREMONY IN THE CIRCLE OF LIFE
Author: White Deer of Autumn
Illustrator: Daniel San Souci
32 pages, $6.95 softbound, ages 6-10

The story of nine-year-old "Little Turtle," a young Native American boy growing up in the city without knowledge of his ancestors' beliefs. He is visited by "Star Spirit," who introduces him to his heritage and his relationship to all things in the "Circle of Life." Little Turtle also learns about nature and how he can help to heal the Earth.

THE GREAT CHANGE
Author: White Deer of Autumn
Illustrator: Carol Grigg
32 pages, $14.95 hardbound, ages 3-10

A Native American tale in which a wise grandmother explains the meaning of death, or the Great Change, to her questioning granddaughter. This is a story of passing on tradition, culture, and wisdom to the next generation. It is a moving tale for everyone who wonders about what lies beyond this life. Watercolor illustrations by internationally acclaimed painter Carol Grigg.

COYOTE STORIES FOR CHILDREN: TALES FROM NATIVE AMERICA
Author: Susan Strauss
Illustrator: Gary Lund
50 pages, $10.95 hardbound, $6.95 softbound, ages 6-12

Storyteller Susan Strauss has interspersed Native American coyote tales with true-life anecdotes about coyotes and Native wisdom. These stories illustrate the creative and foolish nature of this popular trickster and show the wisdom in Native American humor. Whimsical illustrations throughout.